PRAISE FOR *STILL DESERT*

Still Desert knows the wounds of empire have left us collectively "border- / broken, language / lost." Yet, Daniel Elias Galicia is undeterred with a tender vision that bends imagery and texture to guide us, how "ladders / can be toys / like soccer balls / can be water jugs" become truths that weave between erasure and archive, loss and survival. Simultaneously formal and inventive, Galicia attunes and shapeshifts to the ancestral knowing of the flora, the fauna, and the landscape itself to transmute border into a portal. *Still Desert* is a new perception to slowness, to look so deeply that children playing across a border wall teeter-totter "blur" what divides into a proximal memory that "revives."

– Anthony Cody, *The Rendering*

Rooted in the desert, where the "river was once / the border" and where the "sun's a / rattlesnake" for those migrating from one home to another, these poems not only bear witness but remind readers witnessing is a craft. Daniel Elias Galicia is a gifted poet whose lines radiate with music and intuition, who activates the field of the page, who utilizes a wide range of influences and experiences. His poems are borderlands. *The Odyssey*, grief, Yi Sang, the Bath Riots, Colectivo Chopeke, bewilderment, the El Paso Shooting, and survival ripple through and shape the language. These are resonant and beautifully built poems. They moved me deeply.

– Eduardo C. Corral, *Guillotine*

Still Desert examines a place that's "border-broken" and "language-lost." It begins with an emotionally intimate prayer in an old lineage from a different desert where the inhabitants also longed for love and union. Formally in some poems, the lines themselves break apart, integrity degraded by boundaries meant to shatter and scatter. In *Still Desert*, we are reminded that even the horizon is a border. To meditate on the binaries in this collection heightens our desire, rage, loss, even distraction. The poignant "Libélulas" asks us to reflect on this because "the fragile transparencies between us [are] iridescent only in reflected light." These poems leave us thirsty, threatened in our own deserts by what is aggressive and withheld, yet universally understood in our common language of longing. In the desert, we are asked to be still to be renewed in the wash of rain water "cleansing like baptism." This poetry revives in all of us "a sense of home and makes [us] whole again." Though it's still desert, Galicia makes borders transparent to point out where we meet.

– Jeanine Hathaway, *Long After Lauds*

Still Desert is a dynamic debut collection by Daniel Elias Galicia on the varied Mexican American/Chicanx experience in contemporary America. Galicia skillfully paints of social prejudices and struggles, assimilation and racism, identity and culture, familial joy and cultural pride. The collection muses on the subtle nuances of contemporary Chicanx identity while also acknowledging historic and still-present working-class struggles and experiences of Mexican Americans. Galicia's unique storytelling is image-rich with a lush language and has ample range and yet specificity, duende yet a meticulous craft. Galicia proves to be an exciting poet to watch in the American and Mexican American literary landscape and culture. Well done, poet!

– Jose Hernandez Diaz, *Bad Mexican, Bad American*

STILL DESERT

STILL DESERT

poems by:
Daniel Elias Galicia

Button Publishing Inc.
Minneapolis
2025

STILL DESERT
POETRY
AUTHOR: Daniel Elias Galicia
COVER ART: Eric Manuel Santoscoy-Mckillip
COVER DESIGN: Victoria Alvarez

◊

ALL RIGHTS RESERVED

© 2025 by Daniel Elias Galicia

◊

Published by Button Poetry
Minneapolis, MN 55418 | http://www.buttonpoetry.com

◊

Manufactured in the United States of America
PRINT ISBN: 978-1-63834-133-8
EBOOK ISBN: 978-1-63834-127-7

First printing

TABLE OF CONTENTS

Lineage: A Desert Prayer	1
Border Cantos	5
Degradation	9
Águila del desierto	13
Riverless	15
Waiting	16
Coyote's-Eye View	18
Bath Riots, 1917	20
The Sun, Chambered	22
CD. JUAREZ / LA BIBLIA ES / LA VERDAD / LEELA	24
Desert Music	26
"Build the Wall"	29
Drinking with Antonio in Gràcia	35
Libélulas	36
Simulations	37
Ash Wednesday at Ricky's	38
English Literature	39
Apology to #10	41
E1 Buck Private: Amarillo, Texas, 1963	42
Teeter-Totter Wall	45
Sunbreaks	46
Petrichor	49

Notes	53
Acknowledgements	55
About the Author	59
Author Book Recommendations	61
Credits	67

STILL DESERT

Sometimes I think my tongue is a desert praying for rain.

Benjamin Alire Sáenz

LINEAGE: A DESERT PRAYER

We come to you in fear,
        still desert, ghosts & war
behind us, men with guns.
           Let us cross your river,
mother on horseback, thin
               ropes in hand. Give us your
arroyo paths, your desert
          sands: we are border-
broken,   language-
                              lost.
Heartbeat of native lands,
        birth us in blue moonlight.
Desert inside us, hearts
          filled with sand, we walk across you,
our wrinkled faces: etched stones—
            Desert Mother, Desert Father,
                welcome us home.

BORDER CANTOS

After Richard Misrach / Guillermo Galindo

1. Efigie | Effigy

Which road brought you here?
    It's straight but curved:
    a moon half-covered by shade.

Did ghosts haunt you
as you crossed the desert?
    Their footsteps ground gravel,
    shifting rocks the way wind
    shifts leaves.

Pain—I imagine too much pain.
    Wind hollering
    through silence.

What drew you on?
    Coyotes & coyotes.

Do desert ghosts speak?
    Our breaths wheeze on
    plastic Gatorade bottles.

What did you see as you crossed?
    Broken jawbones of cows.
    White scars on rocks.
    Bullets in soccer balls.
    Abandoned clothes
    on effigies
    with outstretched arms.

20 days in the desert...?
>...*20 years to get home.*

Family...?
>...*sounds like wind chimes
on a breezy front porch.*

What do the ghosts look like?
>*Faceless bodies
white as moonlight.*

What is your name?
>*My name is scattered
on pages torn
from a Bible.*

Pain—*hollering wind*
Family—*wind chimes*
Ghosts—*the moonlight reflected
>on the desert,*   (remember me)
>*like an un-remembering sea.*

2. Cucarachas | Cockroaches

Wings. Thorax. Antenna.

The sun scurries
across the sky,

scratches
our skin
red as sand. Heat

like fire ants
on the ripped
carcass
of a rabbit.

No water,
only wind
& the rocks

shattered
like bones.

We stitch
our clothes
with cactus spines.

Our sand-whipped heels
burn. The sun, like

a cockroach,
nicks
the backs
of our necks.

3. Cosas de niños | Children's Things

Aluminum ladders
        can be toys
  like soccer balls
          can be water jugs

              once your coyote's
              stabbed holes in them.

How children play,

                  picking music
            from broken teeth
                of a hairbrush.

Twisted sheets of metal,
    the original toy fence.

  A toothbrush
   can be a toy like gum
    can be money—

     Cállate! he yells—

& hunger is necessary
  as tampons.

    Next day, we find scorpions
   red as blood in
    a trash can riddled
  with bullets. How little

  imagination children need

picking scorpions from
their teeth
  with tweezers.

UNIVERSAL DEGRADATION OF HUMAN RIGHTS

"Be not forgetful to entertain strangers:
for thereby some have entertained angels unawares."
— Hebrews 13:2

the foundation of

disregard and contempt   in
a world in which human beings   enjoy

tyranny and oppression,

the United

States   in cooperation with the

fundamental

Assembly, Proclaims
keeping

peoples   under their jurisdiction.

human beings   born   in
another

race, colour, sex, language, religion

shall   on the basis of political
governing or   other limitation

to life, liberty and the security of person

9

be held in   prohibited   forms

or   inhuman or degrading   punishment

as a person

in violation of

the   national

arbitrary

impartial tribunal,

charged
guilty   in a public trial

on account of any
omission   .

family, home
honour and reputation   has   interference

within the
borders
to leave
to his country.

asylum
may not be invoked   or

the right
shall be arbitrarily deprived   denied   .

nationality or religion
at its dissolution.
only the
fundamental group   is entitled to protection

in association with
his property.

religion
in public

expression
without interference

through any media
has the right
to belong

in the government   or
public
authority   expressed in   elections
held by secret
voting procedures

through national effort and international co-operation
with the   resources of each State   .

employment
without   equal pay for equal work
and

the   limitation of
a standard of living

and

education shall be compulsory

the kind of education given to children

to participate in the cultural and moral interests of the

entitled

community in which is possible

the limitations of morality and democratic society

aimed at the destruction of rights and freedoms.

ÁGUILA DEL DESIERTO

> *"so once again he would heave, would struggle to thrust it up,*
> *sweat drenching his body, dust swirling above his head."*
> — The Odyssey, Book XI: The Kingdom of the Dead

Because he found
    brother, cousin
        facedown.

Because he lost
    home like bones lose
        flesh. Nights, he sits

in bed, stitches
    his heart with cactus
        spines, the muscle

thick, leather-bound.
    Some days he feels
        wind rip pages

from his book of
    longing, pin them
        to barbed wire.

Some days he can't
    go on, lets heat
        blister through him

like water dumped
    by la migra
        from matte black jugs.

Because he can't
   go on, he must
      go on. Father

taught him sun's a
   rattlesnake. *Cover*
      your neck, mijo,

heat's venom. Still
   the nation, like the sun,
      flares up, rears back,

          strikes—

bodies stagger
   to underbrush.
      How to go on

searching for the
   missing, planting
      white crosses for

their remains, up
   & down sun-stroked
      valleys, knowing

the desert, like
   a vulture, claims
      the flesh of bones?

RIVERLESS

"He rebuketh the sea, and maketh it dry, and drieth up all the rivers."
— *Nahum 1:4*

In the desert, rivers
                disappear. When we were young,

        children from both sides played
            in the water. Now wind

            ricochets like a bow,
lifting dust   across strings   of sand.

    How long was I gone? Last time, the river
was here,   & you were here,

        but I can't hold you anymore
            the way deserts can't hold water.

The river was once
    the border

        of our identities. Today, I find myself
                riverless.
  Like time, the Rio Grande
        has dried up: memories
            of you

    now a riverbed of thirst, a bloodline
           trickling away.

    Why did I leave
        like water, dammed
                the river home
                  until you were gone?

WAITING

As mother lies dying
        in the living room

under a morphine dream,
        her hands swell with

pulp, her thin grape
        skin perspires. She's not

my mother anymore:
        eyelids bat open,

pupils, like beetles,
        panic beneath each lens,

moans press her head
        into pillows. She chokes

on her own life.
        Am I a horrible daughter

to wish the owl
        at her window finally

takes flight, her breath
        in its wings? Lord,

when it's my time, let me
        go out with small goodbyes,

like grandfather who walked
        to the porch for one last

flower of cigarette smoke.
        Tonight, as we break down,

struggling with laughter, beers
        on the table, help her let go.

Let her stiff arms have rest.
        Help her fall quietly

as petals into the dark
        waters of your heaven.

COYOTE'S-EYE VIEW

After Yi Sang

13 people wade in the cold river.
(A river black as night in the fenced desert.)

The 1st person crosses the river
  & is terrified.

The 2nd person also crosses the river
    & is terrified.

The 3rd person also crosses the river
      & is terrified.

The 4th person also crosses the river
        & is terrified.

The 5th person also crosses the river
          & is terrified.

The 6th person also crosses the river
          with a baby   & is terrified.

The 7th person is a child carrying a doll
          & she is terrified.

The 8th person is a child carrying a backpack
          & he is terrified.

The 9th person is a child who cannot swim
            & he is terrified.

The 10th person is a child sitting on the 11th person's shoulders
            & they are both terrified.

The 12th person is their coyote wielding a knife
                              & he is terrifying.

The 13th person is also their coyote wielding a gun
                              & he is terrifying.

13 people gasp the cold night air,
                              water up to their waists.

(The stars flicker like flashlights
                              & are terrified or terrifying.)

If the light of 1 star falls in the river
                              it will be alright.

If the light of 2 stars falls in the river
                              it will be alright.

If the light of la migra's flashlights falls in the river
                              will it be alright?

(A river bright with starlight in the open desert.)

BATH RIOTS, 1917

> "Hundreds of dirty lousey [sic] destitute Mexicans arriving at El Paso daily. Will undoubtedly bring and spread typhus unless a quarantine is placed at once."
> — Telegram from El Paso Mayor Tom Lea, Sr., to the U.S. Surgeon General

Our bodies naked, skin
        deloused,

                we wait in line
           at border fumigation sites:

                    eyes lifted,   toxic fumes.

Cruel blades
                shave scalps:

        mothers, daughters,
        fathers, sons.

Our stripped clothes separated, soaked
                    in gasoline baths.

Health officials snap pics
        of breasts through peepholes, post
     their shots, when drunk at night,
                    on cantina walls.

        Months before, immigrant prisoners
        were doused in gas & lit,
          their names

                now wind
          -swept ashes, coyotes' nightly howls.

17-year-old Carmelita Torres says
        no more: women riot,   hurl bottles, stones.

    Outside, the sun's heat runs
        white powder down
    the sky's bared thighs,

            the river a tub
                of crude kerosene.
       We hold our breath, close our eyes:

our lips Zyklon-dusted,
                our pubic hair
                                creosote-clumped.

THE SUN, CHAMBERED

1. 08/03/2019

The desert is a wound
   light's buckshot unheals.
      Here, lizards snap

tails, dart to rocks.
   Today, the sun,
      chambered, rifles

the blue sky, flares:
   another mass
      -ive desert muzzle

flash. Sky-bright silence
   after the blast.
      People like lizards

dart to racks. Punctured
   bags of cereal
      burst in Walmart

aisles. Mesas
   flatline. The hummingbird
      of my heart batters

its wings in the caged
   heat of my chest
      while hate's orchestra

tunes its strings, lifts
   from my throat
      a feathered wail.

2. 08/04/2019

Barefoot in arroyo
    sands, arms outstretched,

        bright bells of sunrise
blare: morning's brass

    horns. A breeze lays
        its hands on my shoulders

while glints of light's
    mercy twist like

        wind chimes in mesquite
& wounded clouds

    mourn in dawn light.

CD. JUAREZ / LA BIBLIA ES / LA VERDAD / LEELA

Painted on the mountain in Juárez:
CD. JUAREZ / THE BIBLE IS / THE TRUTH / READ IT

1.

Did God lose this territory
        long ago? Why else would drug lords

dump bodies ripped by lead
        at church porticos in broad daylight?

Young men machine-gunned down: blue-green flies
        on sun-cracked lips. Yesterday, windstorms

raised a ribcage from the sand & children gathered,
        ate candy from a vendor.

When, for Christ's sake, did death
        become our daily bread?

As long as guns flow south
        & drugs slip back,

those salt-bleached words on the hillside
        turn stomach pink when the sun sets red.

2.

Soldiers in a white Ford pickup
        parked one block away. Red Beret
Army Unit. I preach from the
        podium: Rehab Center #8.

Drug addicts kneel for salvation.
> *Praise the Lord. Turn your faces toward heaven.* Fifteen minutes begin.
>> Bullets fire in all directions.

Father Valles covers me. Masks.
> Hoods. Fresh clips chambered. People dragged outside. Point-blank range. *The Devil's
>> in the streets.* Fifteen minutes.

The pickup never moved. Fifteen
> minutes. Nine people dead. Not a word.
Lord, send down your angels.
> Will there ever be a word?

DESERT MUSIC

What remains is music: in line to cross
    the bridge from Juárez to El Paso—car horns
        & restarted engines, mufflers pumping
black fumes,
    a child's knuckles at the half-lowered window,

his poor mother's plea; afternoons at mercados—
    the blare of mariachi trumpets,
    beer bottles cracked open, cheers

for the man vending his electric shock box; nights on the strip—

    how the DJ's techno thumps
        made us bounce, how we shouted for drinks
            at the bar, asked girls for their names.

But now, daily dissonance changes the music

    of our youth: caesuras like walls

erected; border ballads rewritten
    in keys   of despair.
    From here, we strain
                     to remember songs

once known by heart.

"The border wall threatens the survival of more than 70 plants and animal species."

From "American Scar" — Daniel Lombroso

"BUILD THE WALL"
"BUILD THE WALL"
"BUILD THE WALL"

Golden-cheeked Warbler

California Condor

Mexican Spotted Owl

Least Bell's Vireo

Desert Pupfish   Devils River Minnow

California Gnatcatcher

Bat Nosed Long- Mexican

Checkerspot Butterfly

SAHY Dogweed

Mexican Gray Wolf

New Mexican Ridge-Nosed Rattlesnake

Gulf Coast Jaguarundi

Yaqui Catfish Beautiful Shiner Rio Grande Silvery Minnow Gila Chub Riverside Fairy Shrimp

Guadalupe Fescue

California Orcutt Grass

Cochise Pincushion Cactus

Chiricahua Leopard Frog

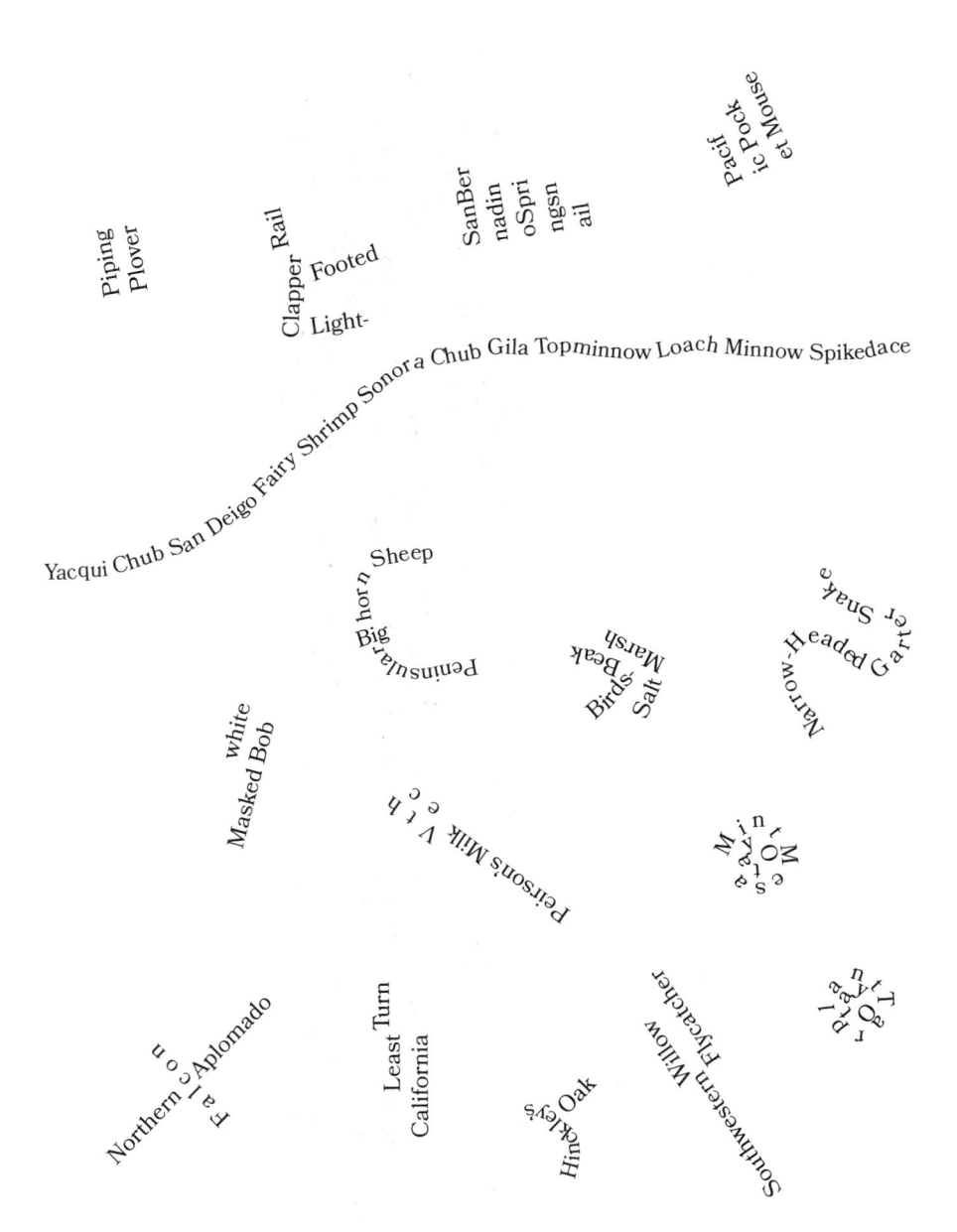

Piping Plover
Clapper Rail
Light-Footed
SanBernadino Springsnail
Pacific Pocket Mouse

Yacqui Chub San Deigo Fairy Shrimp Sonora Chub Gila Topminnow Loach Minnow Spikedace

Bighorn Sheep
Peninsular
Bird's-Beak
Salt Marsh
Narrow-Headed Garter Snake

white Masked Bob
Peirson's Milk Vetch
Mesa Mint

Northern Aplomado Falcon
Least Turn California
Hinckley's Oak
Southwestern Willow Flycatcher
Tuna Playa

31

Mexican Blindcat

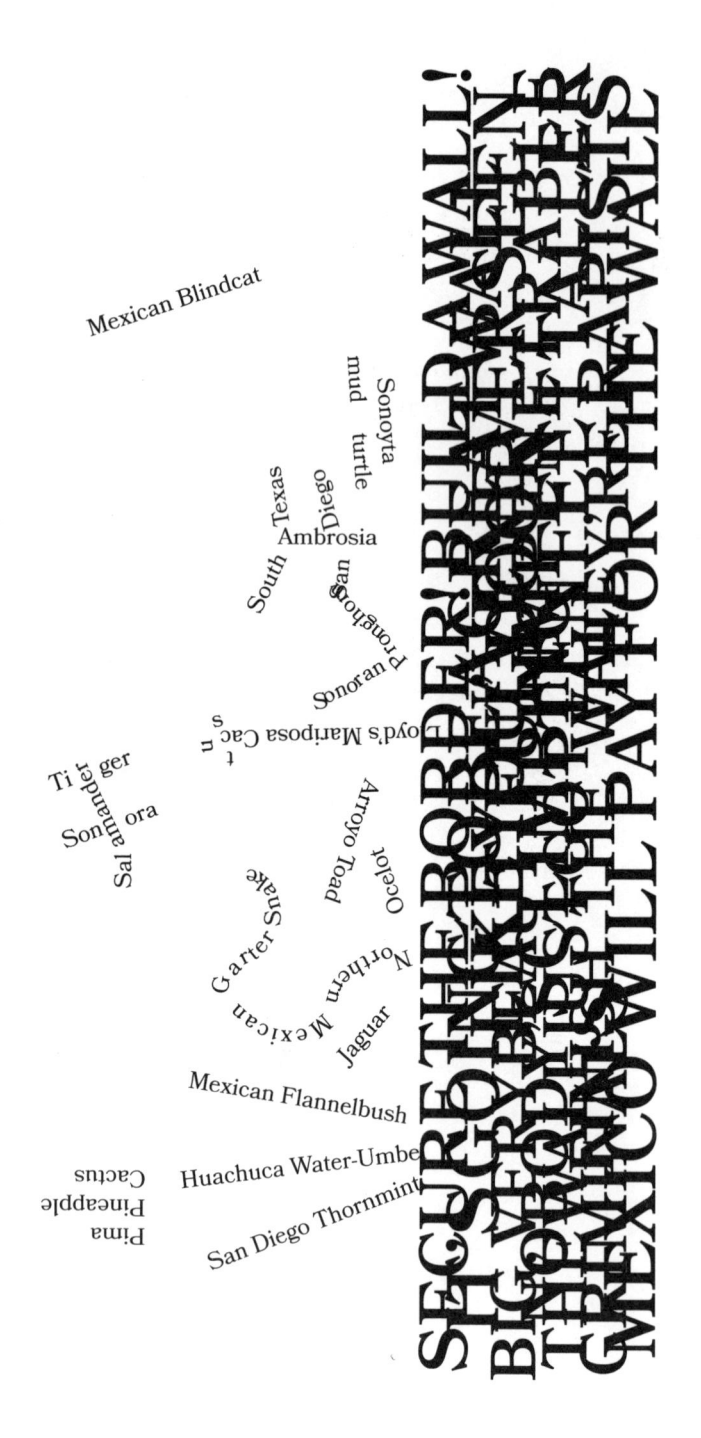

Sonoyta mud turtle

South Texas Ambrosia

San Diego Pogonia

Sonoran Salamander Tiger

Lloyd's Mariposa Cactus

Arroyo Toad

Ocelot

Northern Mexican Garter Snake

Jaguar

Mexican Flannelbush

Pima Pineapple Cactus

Huachuca Water-Umbel

San Diego Thornmint

SECURE THE BORDER! BUILD A WALL!
BIG, BEAUTIFUL, VERY EASY, SEEN
VERY BEAUTIFUL, VERY EASY, SEEN
TREMENDOUSLY BIG NUMBER
GREAT BIG BEAUTIFUL WALL IS
MEXICO WILL PAY FOR THE WALL

DRINKING WITH ANTONIO IN GRÀCIA

"Your laughter frees me . . .
knocks down my cell."
— *Miguel Hernández*

Our two cigarettes, lit & curling smoke,
smolder dimly in the living room, pulsing
light onto sonograms Antonio shows me:
Uma, his daughter, growing silently
without him in another country, warmed
by her mother's blood, while the two of us
clink beers & draw in deeply, listening
to Joan Manuel Serrat sing "Lullaby of the Onion,"
the window frames bending the moonlight.
Between verses, Antonio tells of his grandfather
whom Franco forced by gun into jail, his wife
& child set in hunger's cradle, left to cry out
to whatever God would make onions
taste so bitter.
　　　　　　　While Serrat sings, *Laugh, son,*
you can swallow the moon when you want to,
I see Antonio's tears turn him aside, & somehow
in that moment, I hear my own father crying,
emptying forth prayers through the long nights
of divorce, when the silence from his children
stretched the shadows of his faith. As the song fades,
Antonio keeps humming—his fingers thrumming
his belly, each tap a heartbeat in his ex-wife's womb—
our bands of smoke rising, pressing against
windows, lingering in the pale light like a song.

LIBÉLULAS

As a child, she caught them
near the ditch still known
for its old split tree, tearing
their wings off, giggling
as their bodies fell
to the dry desert grass.
To her they were insects:
numb as leaves, little & strange.
But here in Ascarate Park, our feet
dangling in the lake, she teaches me
the word libélulas as two fly by
clasped in a wheel.
It's been long since we've talked,
yet she finally puts her hand
into mine. She knows
we can be like children:
oblivious to cruelty, unfaithful
to the simplest things
we forget to gently
take hold of, the fragile
transparencies between us
iridescent only in reflected light.

SIMULATIONS

We were only simulations, or so I thought,
in his room locked in blue TV light
where we both shuddered for the first time

like curtains taken by the ceiling fan:
the two of us who for nothing in those late hours
held each other on the roots of our tongues.

ASH WEDNESDAY AT RICKY'S

Recuerda, she says, *que polvo eres*—
her thumb places a cross on my forehead—

y en polvo—blesses me in the language
my parents never taught me, her words blur

in my mind—*te convertirás. Amén.*
Amen, I said, my accent dry as ash,

broken like heritage. *Ricky, please tell
your grandma I can't speak Spanish.*

Entiendo, she replies. But how, I wonder,
can she understand? My parents stopped

their Spanish lullabies when I was three,
grandfather's English Only now complete.

No, she can't understand how I wake
sweating from nightmares, unable to speak,

my tongue absorbed into my body.

ENGLISH LITERATURE

1.

Who here knows how to clean their face, she asked,
standing at the chalkboard. My father—8 years old,

darkest-skinned boy in class in a town of Mexicans—
remembers his classmates' pale eyes. *Homer Brown,*

she called. *Why don't you come up? It seems
your face is dirty.* The teacher's red nails

on his earlobe, he told me, burned hot
while she scrubbed grease from his hairline: fists

clutched to his chest. Silent, they watched his pain-
pressed steps back to his desk. *Now kids, turn*

your books to page 50. Let's read together.
Textbook open, he saw only his hands: sweaty

palms, greasy fingers, skin darkened by sun—
the southwest's dirt disgusting under his fingernails.

2.

In high school, I hid myself in father's books:
literature not in the library—Chicano,

a word I held like a stone, ready to throw. Senior year,
my English teacher assigned poetry recitals. Night

after night, I paced my room, imagined myself
an Aztec Angel, hurled those words against walls,

faced the mirror: proud I was brown, proud
I was my father's son. On performance day,

I stood up front, gripped the page. A classmate
raised her hand. *Why do minorities just complain?*

My teacher nodded. I didn't disagree. Despite
my "Stupid America" recitation, I sat down,

poem in hand: the taste of stone in my busted mouth.

APOLOGY TO #10

Before the game, I heard my coaches talk
about me: how they wished I were like him—

smooth with the ball, draining shots from behind
the three-point line—my brother, the all-city

basketball star, whose jersey hangs from rafters:
numbers pressed into our school's history.

No wonder I stayed in the locker room
at halftime, my team down, & beat my fists

against the metal—their voices ringing
in my head (*Damn it, boy!*)—my knuckles cut

like strips of paper, bones like sharp pencils
punching through. Back on the court, second half,

as I boxed out for a rebound, I let
their words break me like a rubber band &

threw my elbow into #10's face:
his nose a bowl of crunched red cereal.

This poem is my apology. Sorry
I stained your white jersey with blood. While you

were only fighting for possession, I
was losing what it meant to be myself.

E1 BUCK PRIVATE: AMARILLO, TEXAS, 1963

"One of the things which I have taken the greatest interest has been in attempting to pursue an example that was long neglected... to prove that in this hemisphere, from top to bottom, in all of the countries, whether they be Latin or North American, that there is a common commitment to freedom, to equality of opportunity... and to show to the world a very bright star in this country and indeed in the entire hemisphere."
— *President Kennedy, Remarks in Houston, Texas to LULAC*

Viva Kennedy!

Steam rose from the dishwater, hot with grease,
in the bowling alley's kitchen: my part-
time job in town, a few miles off Route 66.
      Mexican food on the menu, no Mexicans around—
just me: my dark hands red in the sink.   Back on the base,

I played trombone for the 584th band.
We played Glen Miller as Air Force cadets
deplaned the B-52s. The first day
I joined, my 1st Sergeant gave me two rules:
one—be clean, private; two—   don't go to Mexican town.

                    At work, the waitress
flirted with me. Her blonde hair flashed
in the empty kitchen. We joked until
someone stepped in.   I watched her carry plates,
talk to customers,   never knowing what they said.

Each 4th, the band played in town parades.
We marched down lanes, turned, marched back.   Once, the band
took a bus from Post, Texas to Lubbock,
stopped for food along the way: the whites got off, took our orders—
we waited on the bus,   the blacks sang songs.

On Wednesdays, I'd go to a country bar
with a guy I knew. He was broad-chested, hard-nosed,
seemed a racist, but we were friends.   Once, the jukebox
kept playing Hank Williams' "Your Cheatin' Heart"
while a drunk private cried at the bar. *That's my life,*

he moaned. *I loved her,*
but she's a bitch.
                              I reached to help.
A cowboy stood, said:
          Know your place, young man.

Later, I asked the blonde waitress out.
She refused.   Said drive-ins were fine, though.
Friday nights, my friend Tom Foard would lend me
his Ford.   There, in gray film light, her blonde hair
was free. She was free. Free enough   to hide.

I didn't know it then:
     my (her) attraction to her (me) was her (an)   embarrassment.
                    I didn't know what to do with that.

Weekdays, I buffed floors on base: wood barrack
floors,   leaned my forearms hard on the handles,
          buffed until the floor's luster shone, buffed until
someone stepped in.   *You'd better come.*   In a small room
near the offices, a small TV in the corner,
all the privates, secretaries huddled in silence. That was the Friday
                    Kennedy was shot.

I stood behind the group, tears in my eyes,
the hope I had (we had) in him (for him) for us,   died too.
I didn't know what to do with that.   I went back, buffed,
buffed, polished the wood, mad
someone had stepped in, left their shoe prints on
                                        my clean, clean floor.

TEETER-TOTTER WALL

"Recognize yourself in he and she who are not like you and me."
— *Carlos Fuentes*

Pink as cotton candy

seesaws straddle the border.

Girls & boys bounce,

laughter lilts through

slits in the fence.

These toys turn walls

into illusion,

our zeitgeist zoetrope spun.

With every swing,

bars blur.

SUNBREAKS

    Hope is a wind

        -blown cloud:

            it changes shapes,

evaporates,

      colors desert mountains

          with sunbreaks.

PETRICHOR

When rain returns
    to drought-weary
deserts, the earth
    signals its arrival:

a scent released
    from sun-blazed sand
& chaparral
    rises like praise—

nature's censers
    perfuming arroyo
sanctuaries,
    where ocotillo,

blossom-less, dry,
    reach spiny arms
to skies, as thirst,
    their prayer, is answered

once sheet-like clouds
    stretch shade
before the sun's
    fiery defiance;

a fragrance light
    as a breeze, pure
as god blood, cleansing
    like baptism: a blessing

short-lived. This scent
          my ancestors sought
for survival,
          revives in me,

no matter the distance,
          my withered sense
of home & makes
          it whole again.

button poetry

NOTES

Epigraph: From "Meditation on Living in the Desert" (No. 17), in *The Book of What Remains* by Benjamin Alire Sáenz. (Copper Canyon Press, 2010).

"Border Cantos": Title & sub-titles are borrowed from *Border Cantos* by Richard Misrach & Guillermo Galindo. (Aperture, 2016).

"Degradation" is an erasure poem drawn from the text of the Universal Declaration of Human Rights. Epigraph is from the King James Bible.

"Águila del desierto": Inspired by both the selfless, Sisyphean acts of the volunteer group Águilas del Desierto & the Rolling Stone article "The Deadliest Crossing" by Jason Motlagh. Epigraph is a description of Sisyphus from Robert Fagles' translation of *The Odyssey* (Penguin Classics, 1999).

"Riverless": Dedicated to the memory of Annette Franco. Epigraph is from the King James Bible.

"Coyote's-Eye View": After Yi Sang's "Crow's-Eye View" (Poem No. 1) in *Three Poets of Modern Korea* translated by Yu Jung-Yul & James Kimbrell (Sarabande Books, 2002).

"Bath Riots, 1917": Epigraph found in David Dorado Romo's *Ringside Seat to a Revolution: An Underground Cultural History of El Paso and Juárez: 1893-1923* (Cinco Punto Press, 2005). Thank you, Mr. Romo, for the inspiration your work has provided & for your kind support.

"The Sun, Chambered": Dedicated to those who lost their lives in the 2019 El Paso shooting. El Paso Strong.

"CD. JUAREZ / LA BIBLIA ES / LA VERDAD / LEELA": Based on true events surrounding the massacre at CIAD #8 in Juárez on 8/13/2008.

"Desert Music": The poem's form is borrowed, with variations, from "Providence" by Natasha Trethewey in *Native Guard*.

"Build the Wall": Epigraph from Daniel Lombroso's 2022 New Yorker documentary *American Scar*. Title is borrowed, as a critique, from Trump's 2016 presidential campaign political slogan. List of at-risk animals & plants threatened by Trump's border wall is found at the end of *American Scar*. Overlaid wall of text are all tweets & statements from Trump about the border.

"Drinking with Antonio in Gràcia": Epigraph from "Lullaby of the Onion" by Miguel Hernández. The phrase "hunger's cradle" is borrowed from "Lullaby of the Onion."

"English Literature": The phrase "Aztec Angel" refers to Luis Omar Salinas' poem "Aztec Angel." The poem "Stupid America" was written by Abelardo "Lalo" Delgado.

"E1 Buck Private: Amarillo, Texas, 1963": Epigraph from JFK's visit with Latino civil rights leaders the night before his death, Nov. 21, 1963. The slogan "Viva Kennedy!" drove JFK to win 85% to 90% of the Latino vote in 1960.

"Teeter-Totter Wall": Epigraph from Mexican writer Carlos Fuentes, 1928-2012. Inspired by the art installation "Teeter-Totter Wall" from artists Ronald Rael & Virginia San Fratello with Colectivo Chopeke.

ACKNOWLEDGMENTS

To my dear wife: thank you for always believing in me.

To my parents & family: your unconditional love and support are pure blessings.

To my mentors Jeanine & Jeanne: what good grace brought such wonderfully nurturing teachers into my life? You are both so dear to me.

To my friends & fellow artists: your presence in my life sustains me. A big, warm abrazo to Eric, Chris, Mike, and Jo Anna.

A very big thank you to the following publications for first publishing several of the poems in this collection:

Askew, Beloit Poetry Journal, Button Poetry, *EcoTheo Review, Iron Horse Literary Review, MEZCLA: Art & Writings from the Tumblewords Project, Pyrta Journal, Relief: A Journal of Art & Faith,* and *Ruminate.*

Finally, I would like to gratefully acknowledge the wonderful team at Button Poetry for believing in these poems. Thank you, in particular, to Tanesha Kozler & Charley Eatchel for your generous work developing & editing the collection.

If you care to make a donation to help provide high-quality legal services to low-income immigrants or help families whose loved ones are missing in the desert near our border, please visit https://las-americas.org & https://aguilasdeldesierto.org.

ABOUT THE AUTHOR

Daniel Elias Galicia is the son of Chicana/o activists & educators. He is from El Paso, Texas & holds an MFA in Creative Writing. His poems have appeared in *Beloit Poetry Journal*, Button Poetry, *EcoTheo Review, Ruminate Magazine, Iron Horse Literary Review, Relief: A Journal of Art & Faith,* & more. He is a Pushcart-nominated poet & the recipient of an Editor's Choice Award from *Relief.*

AUTHOR BOOK RECOMMENDATIONS

How to Maintain Eye Contact by Robert Wood Lynn

In *How to Maintain Eye Contact*, Robert Wood Lynn observes a world where we prefer to look ourselves straight in the eyes and lie: we lie to ourselves that cell phones, the internet, and airplanes are more sacred than a rare snow owl; that elves and heaven are more real than the final moments we share with our loved ones and friends; that the rules guiding our ordinary lives are more important, even as we let "the future burn / its fossil fuel of the plausibly deniable." Lynn's art is one of subtle wordsmanship, though his message is anything but subtle. As the world burns, this book becomes its own "way of holding" all the beauty of a humanity equally capable of tender love and numb destruction. Look into the eyes of everything you love and hold that eye contact, Lynn suggests, for as he sees it, unless things change, "we're goners." And that's the truth.

Smut Psalm by Josh Tvrdy

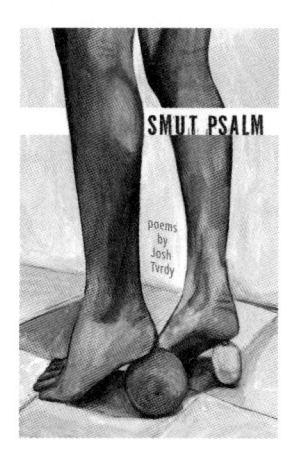

The title says it all: *Smut Psalm*. This collection is an exercise in deftly crafted juxtaposition—or "scandalous union," as Josh Tvrdy writes, who believes that "things change when they touch"—a concept that plays out in every layer of craft, leaving the reader changed as well. These poems bring to the forefront the oft-hushed cruelties lurking behind the veneer of Christian upbringings, putting them on full display. As you read this collection, you weep for the innocent young boy who yearns for simple fatherly affection, rejoice in his ardent stance of independence, and linger on questions of what it means to exist in contradiction to something you both love and hate.

Birthright by George Abraham

Birthright is beautifully written and heartbreakingly relevant. In this collection, Abraham uses dynamic poetic forms to evoke historical erasure, generational trauma, and the remapping of "unwritten people." With volcanic energy, these poems erupt on the page, questioning with righteous indignation why a state has the right to determine who deserves to exist. Without flinching, Abraham delivers hard-hitting truths, offering a powerful collection that explores how religion, language, countries, people, history, and politics fail us, searching endlessly for what we can rely on and find hope in.

CREDITS

Assistant Editors
Amina Ahmed
Reese Brunette
Melanie Koopmans
Rabi Michael-Crushshon
Isabelle Miller
Destanee Ulrich

Book Photography
Emily Van Cook

Cover and Interior Design
Victoria Alvarez
Charley Eatchel
Isabelle Miller
Eric Manuel Santoscoy-Mckillip

Distribution
SCB Distributors

Ebook Production
Siva Ram Maganti

Editor
Charley Eatchel

Publisher
Sam Van Cook

Publishing Operations Manager
TaneshaNicole Kozler

Publishing Operations Assistant
Charley Eatchel

Social Media and Marketing
Catherine Guden
Isabelle Miller
Eric Tu

OTHER BOOKS BY BUTTON POETRY

If you enjoyed this book, please consider checking out some of our others, below. Readers like you allow us to keep broadcasting and publishing. Thank you!

Rachel Wiley, *Revenge Body*
Ebony Stewart, *BloodFresh*
Ebony Stewart, *Home.Girl.Hood.*
Kyle Tran Myhre, *Not A Lot of Reasons to Sing, but Enough*
Steven Willis, *A Peculiar People*
Topaz Winters, *So, Stranger*
Darius Simpson, *Never Catch Me*
Blythe Baird, *Sweet, Young, & Worried*
Siaara Freeman, *Urbanshee*
Robert Wood Lynn, *How to Maintain Eye Contact*
Junious 'Jay' Ward, *Composition*
Usman Hameedi, *Staying Right Here*
Sean Patrick Mulroy, *Hated for the Gods*
Sierra DeMulder, *Ephemera*
Taylor Mali, *Poetry By Chance*
Matt Coonan, *Toy Gun*
Matt Mason, *Rock Stars*
Miya Coleman, *Cottonmouth*
Ty Chapman, *Tartarus*
Lara Coley, *ex traction*
DeShara Suggs-Joe, *If My Flowers Bloom*
Ollie Schminkey, *Where I Dry the Flowers*
Edythe Rodriguez, *We, the Spirits*
Topaz Winters, *Portrait of My Body as a Crime I'm Still Committing*
Zach Goldberg, *I'd Rather Be Destroyed*
Eric Sirota, *The Rent Eats First*
Neil Hilborn, *About Time*
Josh Tvrdy, *Smut Psalm*
Phil SaintDenisSanchez, *before & after our bodies*
Ebony Stewart, *WASH*
L.E. Bowman, *Shapeshifter*
Najya Wiliams, *on a date with disappointment*
Jalen Eutsey, *Bubble Gum Stadium*
Meg Ford, *Wild/Hurt*
Jared Singer, *Forgotten Neccessities*

Available at buttonpoetry.com/shop and more!

BUTTON POETRY BEST SELLERS

Neil Hilborn, *Our Numbered Days*
Hanif Abdurraqib, *The Crown Ain't Worth Much*
Olivia Gatwood, *New American Best Friend*
Sabrina Benaim, *Depression & Other Magic Tricks*
Melissa Lozada-Oliva, *peluda*
Rudy Francisco, *Helium*
Rachel Wiley, *Nothing Is Okay*
Neil Hilborn, *The Future*
Phil Kaye, *Date & Time*
Andrea Gibson, *Lord of the Butterflies*
Blythe Baird, *If My Body Could Speak*
Rudy Francisco, *I'll Fly Away*
Andrea Gibson, *You Better Be Lightning*
Rudy Francisco, *Excuse Me As I Kiss The Sky*

Available at buttonpoetry.com/shop and more!